KIDS SPACES

images Publishing

KIDS SPACES

Architecture for Children

FURNITURE

Easel + Art Cart
• Kids' Studioworks

Kids' Studiowork's Alla Kazovsky believes that children are natural artists. The easel and art cart places within easy reach all the supplies and tools a young artist would need, so that kids can explore their own creativity. Everything is on hand whenever the creative spark arises.

Durable, shatter-proof white plastic forms the structure that holds work surfaces of clear acrylic (clipboard) and marker board. Circular cut-outs add interest as well as function—they are suitable for storage for rolls of paper and finished artwork. Translucent red, yellow, and blue acrylic form trays and drawers to hold art supplies, and keep the area tidy.

Work surfaces are independently adjustable to accommodate children of varying ages (from toddlers to teenagers). All necessary fasteners are included for easy assembly.

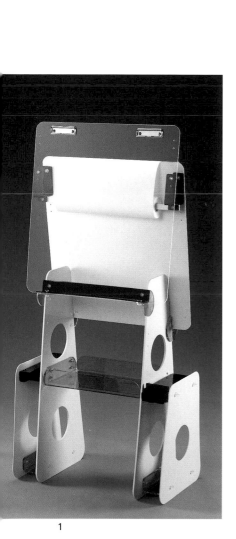

1

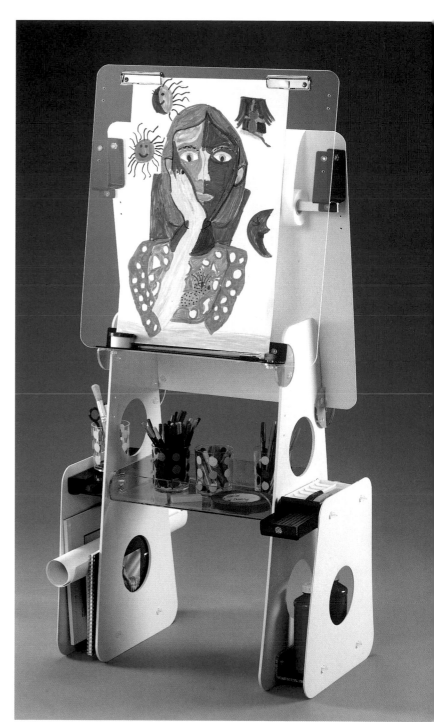

2

Jewel Box of Bombay Bedroom
Los Angeles Home, Pacific Palisades, California, USA
• Chris Barrett

Romantic notions of the Shangri La are present in Chris Barrett's design for a teenage girl's India-inspired bedroom.

The walls are a soft, caramel colored Venetian plaster with an Indian motif etched in the ceiling.

Barrett's design for the bed was inspired by a motif often found on doors and niches in India. The headboard has a secret compartment in which a diary, for example, can be hidden.

A bright and colorful antique rug sits atop the wide-planked antiqued oak, and crisp bed linens complement the custom-made Indian sari duvet cover and decorative pillows.

The study tower features custom-made, Barrett-designed benches using antique yogi legs. The benches are covered with saris and custom-woven pillows.

The tower's domed ceiling has been bronzed, and a bejeweled Moroccan lantern hangs from the center.

In the bathroom, Barrett found an old rice trunk and turned it into the bathroom vanity unit. A Moroccan lantern has been added over the bathtub, and a shower curtain fabricated from an Indian sari. The bench is made from an old tilling tool.

1

2

1 *Daughter's room*

2 *Meditation/Study tower*

Drawings: *Jennifer Rimlinger, CBD, Inc.*

Pacific Palisades Home
Pacific Palisades, California, USA
• Kids' Studioworks

1

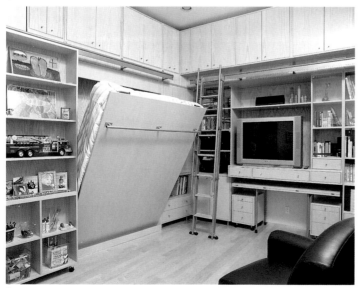

2

3

By designing two children's rooms and a family room, Alla Kazovsky created a safe, practical, and stimulating environment. This thoughtful design adopts a holistic approach that also introduces chemical-free standards.

The custom-designed children's beds, with built-in storage and mobility in mind, have headboards that can be reconfigured, shelves, and drawers. The shelving is double-sided, and the wheeled display case doubles as a collection cart.

The living space, or 'Kitchen of the Mind' provides an area in the house for projects, library, media, storage, and guest bedding. Its floor-to-ceiling cabinets are open and glass fronted. It also has a sliding bookcase, stepladder, pull-out table or desk, and roll-out chest.

The environment's safety is enhanced with the use of natural-fiber linen and fleece blan-

4

5

kets, formaldehyde-free glues and plywoods, pigment-free wall and ceiling paints, and clear-finished woods. The flooring is made from plywood with a water-based polyurethane finish, with a noticeable absence of floor coverings.

RETAIL

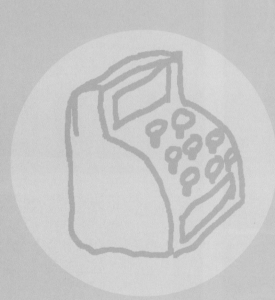

Atom & Eve

Toronto, Ontario, Canada
• II BY IV Design
Associates, Inc

1

2

3

4

1 *Traffic-stopping storefront design reveals more fun inside*

2 *Toys and TV center for kids; streamlined displays for their parents*

3 *Out of the clear blue sky, bright green apples!*

4 *Merchandising wall's concealed standards facilitate clothing display*

Photography: *David Whittaker*

This new retail concept is neat, clean and crisp—just like a bright green apple.

The up-market children's footwear outlet is in a shopping environment that is safe and refreshing for kids and their parents.

A huge overscale graphic of green apples forms a dramatic backdrop to the sales desk, and, as in the front window, small display cubbies are mounted against it. On either side of the main aisle, above small carpeted areas, cove-lit recessed ceiling niches reveal a blue sky glimpsed, in a child's-eye view, from below the branches of a heavily laden apple tree. And sure enough, in dynamic mobiles suspended from the center of the niches, bright green apples 'fall' to earth—or more accurately to just above the bowls of tasty real apples that form the centerpiece of the display cubes below.

Located on a corner, the second storefront at the narrow end calls for a second dramatic back wall feature of a giant green apple graphic flanked by oversized, backlit images of a lively boy and girl. Below it is centered a large-screen television where video movies and cartoons keep small shoppers entertained while their siblings are being fitted. Those unused to sitting still can feel free to clamber over the tiers of benches flanking the set, and inhabited by dozens of furry stuffed toys.

From the board game-like pattern of the vinyl flooring with its extra-wide aisles, to the full barrier-free washroom and baby change room, this open and welcoming store is comfortable and obstacle-free for parents, tots, baby carriages, and rambunctious youngsters alike. It's bright, practical, witty and utterly charming, much like the beautifully designed merchandise it displays.

Outtakes at ABN AMRO Retail Arcade

Chicago, Illinois, USA

• Vasilko . Hauserman & Associates, Inc.

1

In this instance, children influence the corporate culture.

ABN AMRO is a progressive institution that cares for the needs of its employees and their families. The heart of this urban financial setting is a place for children to enjoy and for adults to frequent. Outtakes is a store in the retail arcade that caters to a variety of needs including those of children. The Kids Zone is a little piece of wonderland with all the trimmings of toys and confections. Inviting and playful, the store encourages children to spend time trying out the goods. Adults have been known to do so too.

The accent is on design at this hip new boutique in the West Loop. Outtakes is the place to find one-of-a-kind gifts from emerging artists and designers. The Outtakes collection offers contemporary, fashionable accessories and gifts.

2

The Kids Zone is a retail program element required by the ABN AMRO employees, who expressed their need for this store feature by way of a programming survey. Flik International Corporation, Outtakes, and Vasilko . Hauserman's design team developed retail station concepts for each focus point of the survey. The store reflects the eclectic nature of the offerings.

1 *The Kids Zone—a little piece of wonderland*

2 *Hip new boutique in Chicago's West Loop*

3 *Outtakes floor plan*

4 *All the trimmings of toys and confections*

Photography:
Vasilko . Hauserman & Associates, Inc.

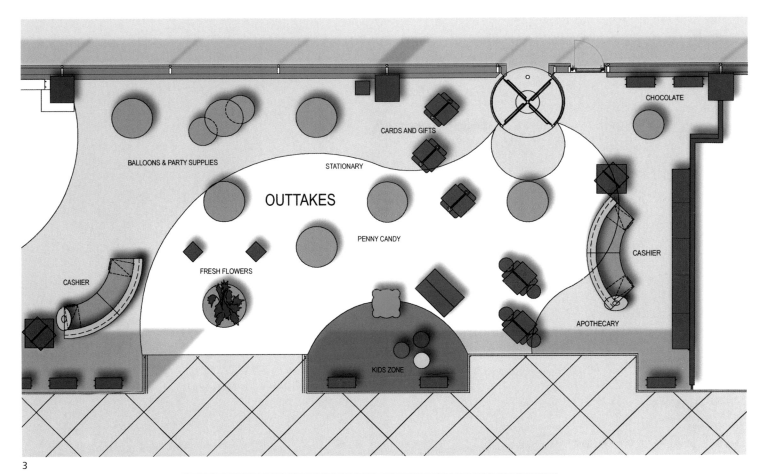

BALLOONS & PARTY SUPPLIES

CARDS AND GIFTS

CHOCOLATE

STATIONARY

OUTTAKES

PENNY CANDY

CASHIER

FRESH FLOWERS

CASHIER

APOTHECARY

KIDS ZONE

3

4

DAYCARE

JCC in Manhattan
New York, New York, USA
• Diamond & Schmitt Architects Incorporated
in association with Schuman Lichtenstein Clamon Efron Architects

Located on the second level of the new 11-story community center, the nursery school is a collection of eight light-filled rooms organized around a large common space. The common space is the heart of the nursery school where the children display their artwork, participate in story time or music classes, and perform plays. The front wall of the common space integrates a commissioned art installation comprising an aquarium, terrarium, and sculptural pieces depicting an allegorical tale of evolution. A retractable projection screen and audio-visual equipment allow for multimedia presentations.

>>

1 *Rooftop terrace playground*

2 *Looking toward aquarium/
terrarium hall*

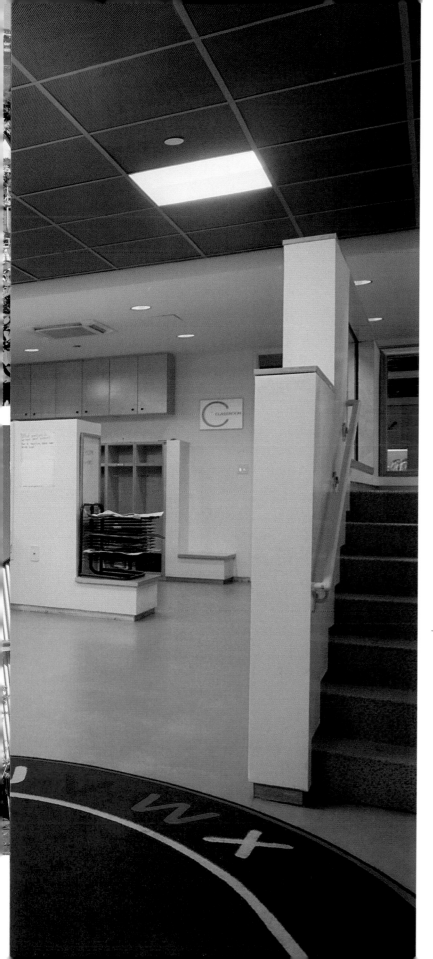

4

The classrooms are simple in plan. Natural maple millwork helps to define and sculpt the space into three zones: an entry with personalized cubbies for clothing and storage; a quiet loft and interior zone for teaching, reading, and exploring; and an active, open play zone at the perimeter.

The palette of natural materials and neutral tones is balanced by accents of bright colors. All the furniture and plumbing fixtures are scaled for infants.

Opposite *Typical classroom*

4 *Common space— artwork display*

Photography: *Steven Evans*

12

13

12 *All shapes are playfully conceived*

13 *Open spaces are easily reconfigured*

14 *Spaces are scaled for children*

15 *Materials are neutral so kids add color*

16 *Windows are placed at child's level*

Photography:
Christian Kandzia/ Behnisch & Partner

14

16

15

Preschool
Paris, France
• Architecture-Studio

1

2

This design for an inner-urban project mixes residential with other functions. Space is included for a preschool for 70 children, 151 residential units and car parking, corporate space, and other office space.

The building's site dictates that it must comply with multiple urban planning schemes, including one that relates to the Seine River.

The architects created a building that is dense yet fragmented to accommodate the different elements, while providing unity to the entire project. The side facing the Seine features bay windows and balconies and presents a ten-story façade. The other façade, looking over Balard Street, maintains an eight-story urban plan.

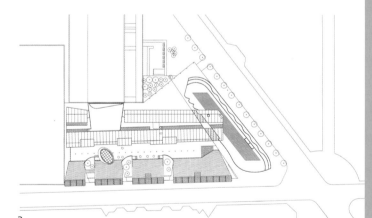

3

1 *Façade*
2 *Block interior*
3 *Site plan*
4 *Preschool atrium*
Photography: *Patrick Tourneboeuf*

4

Winnetka Public School Nursery
Winnetka, Illinois, USA
- ArchitectureIsFun, Inc. and Michael Evans Landscape Architect

1 *Reggio plan as outdoor learning environment*

2 *Parade path is an 'infinite loop' of activity complete with drive-through shed, perfect for tricycles and celebration*

3 *The Hill, with its vista, is a place for reflection or small group play*

The Winnetka Public School Nursery's Outdoor Learning Environment takes its inspiration from trains, tracks, and stations but its philosophies from the curriculum. Striving to foster each child's potential, the outdoor environment is safe, secure and accessible. It is a place where children are free to make choices, to become actively involved in decision-making, and to have physical and cognitive experiences out in the 'open.' In the classrooms, children surround themselves with rich and engaging materials. Taking that concept outside, areas such as the Musical Forest with wind chimes and speaker tubes, the Infinite Loop Tricycle Path with drive-through, the Crazy Box pavilion climbers and the Theme Gardens with their seasonal offerings, were all created to provide interest, challenge, and stimulation.

1

2

3

The Outdoor Learning Environment is an invigorated variant of more traditional, sedate (cookie-cutter) playgrounds seen the world over. Taking its lead from the strong educational philosophies of the nursery and the developmental needs of the children, the Winnetka Public School Nursery's Outdoor Learning Environment is truly an outdoor classroom where children experience nature, science, and art.

5

6

7

8

Opposite *Geometry Land is a place to make sense of physical work by experimenting with water, sand, and a 'big dig'*

5 *Classroom continues out-doors as an emotionally secure environment where children progress at their own pace*

6 *Platform #9 is both a stage and music-making station*

7 *Children riding past can cheer on fellow students who aim for top of climbing wall*

8 *Outdoor art-making and letter writing occurs naturally at pipe structures*

Photography:
Doug Snower Photography

Tsukushi Daycare Center

Yokohama City, Kanagawa Prefecture, Japan

• Environment Design Institute

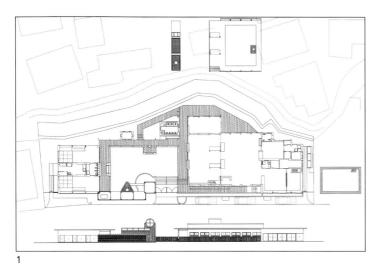

Catering for 60 children, this daycare center has a central courtyard divided into two, with one section for ages under one year, and a section for children aged 2–5 years.

A corridor connects the separate areas.

A tower play structure in the courtyard faces the road, and an air corridor and net play equipment furnish the room for the children aged 3–5 years.

1 *Site plan*

2 *External view of school building*

3 *Tsukushi tower*

4 *Climbing play structure*

5 *Courtyard from the semi-outdoor space*

6 *Classroom and climbing play structure*

7 *Catwalk spaces in classroom are fun for kids*

Photography: *Hiroyuki Oki*

4

5

6

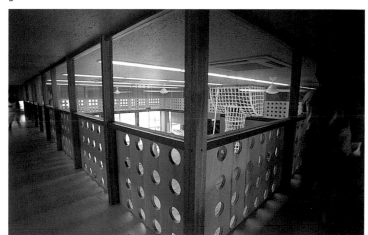

7

Tsukushi Daycare Center | Environment Design Institute   35

Preschool Wing of the Glenview Park Center

Glenview, Illinois, USA

• Williams Architects

1

2

This multi-room preschool carries the architectural design style of the 15,300-square-meter community center of which it is a part.

Williams Architects developed the design of the center's overall structure in the Prairie style, creating harmony with the 60-hectare park surrounding the site.

The exterior of the structure features brick masonry and limestone detailing. To conserve energy, wide roof overhangs were designed, and windows with Low-E glazing installed. The preschool wing, which encompasses approximately 1000 square meters, opens to a fenced outdoor playground.

The wing contains six classrooms, arranged in pairs, with each pair sharing a work/preparation room designed to support teaching activity. Each room is served by a 'child-sized' toilet room.

The wing also incorporates a babysitting room for use by facility patrons, and a room for parent/child activity programs.

Each classroom exits directly to the outdoors as a safety consideration. Learning/play areas feature custom-designed, hand-painted wallpaper and borders.

1 *Preschool wing of prairie-style Glenview Park Center*

2 *Preschool classroom*

Photography:
Robert McKendrick Photography

EDUCATION

2

Eco Learning, Schaeffer Elementary School
Lancaster, Pennsylvania, USA
• Reese Lower Patrick & Scott, Ltd

1

This project involved renovations and additions to a 3250-square-meter elementary school to create a 5900-square-meter innovative learning environment. The new design maintains the building's 1935 character, while incorporating an overall ecology and environmental theme throughout the building. Details include natural finishes of oak woodwork, leaf-patterned counters, and carpeting and classrooms signs with pictures of local plant species.

The renovations increased the capacity of the K–5 school from three to four classrooms per grade, where even core subjects like reading and math are taught through an ecological perspective. Other new features include a hands-on discovery laboratory, observatory station, gymnasium with climbing wall, cafeteria/auditorium, and an octagonal music room. All of the shared spaces are connected to the single-level, central 'Main Street' stately arched, brick hallway.

The renovated school has flexibility, with several multi-purpose spaces and classrooms that can be easily modified to accommodate different activities. The new classrooms feature built-in cabinets with an audio visual unit and sliding dry erase boards, as well as hallway display cabinets to aid wayfinding. Each also provides yet another opportunity to accentuate the ecological learning theme.

The ecological theme is evident on the outside with a man-made eco-courtyard and pond which will be utilized by other students within the district. The 12-meter, 30,000-liter pond and creek hosts a variety of native plant and aquatic life. The eco-garden includes outdoor lighting, seating areas, a wheelchair-accessible path, and interpretive signs. Recently passed legislation for business tax credits helped secure a grant to fund the project.

3

1 *Exterior side view*

2 *New cafeteria/auditorium*

3 *'Main Street' corridor provides access to offices, library, cafeteria, gymnasium, music room, and classroom*

4 *Waterfall*

5 *Eco-garden plan*

6 *Pond grass*

7 *Renovated classroom showing corridor display boxes*

8 *Octagon-shaped music room*

Photography:
Larry Lefever Photography

4

5

6

7

8

1 *Student Center east entrance*
2 *Digital Media Center floor plan*
3 *Student Center interior concourse*
4 *Motion capture studio for creating digital video animation*
5 *Graphics editing lab*

Kids Technology—Where Work and Play are One

Chicago, Illinois, USA

• Vasilko . Hauserman & Associates, Inc.

1

The DePaul University Media Center is located within Chicago's vibrant Lincoln Park neighborhood. The Media Center was developed to foster the tremendous depth of skill and knowledge of children in the neighborhood. The symbiotic relationship of college students to primary grade students is achieved through the use of multimedia technology.

The Media Center provides an opportunity for kids to explore a variety of cutting-edge digital media equipment and environments. Kindergarten through high school students are invited to explore an array of digital technologies through the use of the digital studios and laboratories that comprise the Media Center—a digital playground.

The Media Classroom boasts ergonomic, touch-screen monitors, wireless keyboards, and multimedia projection capabilities. This classroom is the perfect forum for exploring media technique and reviewing kids' projects. A web camera is available to broadcast these productions to the world. Numerous computer stations enable boys and girls to utilize their newly gained knowledge and refine their digital skills. Kids in the Digital Sound Lab enthusiastically create and mix music for manipulation in the digital realm.

A favorite with the children is the Motion Capture Studio. The motion capture suite digitally captures the individual's action to be rendered onto characters or for motion studies in animation. The interplay of technology, digital media, and enthusiastic children stimulates a high level of creativity, cooperation, and learning.

The digital world lives within these kids! Vasilko . Hauserman took the special needs of small children into account when designing and detailing this multi-media extravaganza.

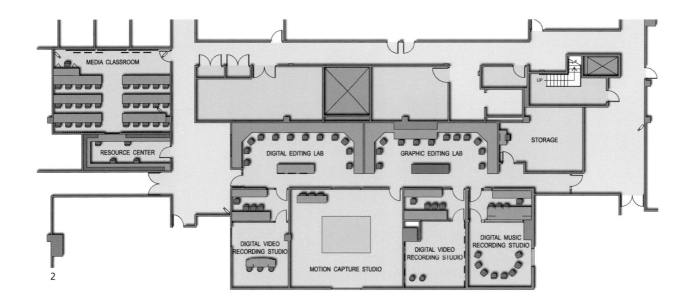

2

MEDIA CLASSROOM

RESOURCE CENTER

DIGITAL EDITING LAB

GRAPHIC EDITING LAB

STORAGE

UP

DIGITAL VIDEO RECORDING STUDIO

MOTION CAPTURE STUDIO

DIGITAL VIDEO RECORDING STUDIO

DIGITAL MUSIC RECORDING STUDIO

3

4

5

7

6

6&7 *Fun in the digital editing lab*

8 *Computer workstations can project onto twin screens*

9 *Digital video recording studio with mock news room*

10 *Instructors not needed; children assist each other*

Photography:
Craig Dugan, Hedrich-Blessing (1&3); Vasilko . Hauserman & Associates, Inc. (2,4–10)

8

9

10

Public School 156 and Intermediate School 392

Brooklyn, New York, USA

• Mitchell/Giurgola Architects, LLP

1

2

Public School 156 and Intermediate School 392 accommodate 1200 students from preschool to eighth grade in the 14,600-square-meter facilities. They serve as magnet schools for academic excellence with a focus on the arts, as well as provide the primary civic building in the community.

The school became the first school in the community for gifted and talented students, and was awarded an arts grant to provide special art classes to enhance its curriculum. Unique to the school are its state of the art gymnasium, a 450-seat auditorium, a journalism studio, a music room with practice cubicles, art suites equipped with a ceramics room, a photography lab with darkroom, a science lab, and a recording studio.

1 *North playground*

2 *Main entrance off Legion Street*

3 *West elevation of new facilities showing community context*

4 *Exterior view from playground of two-story wall art by sculptor Ned Smyth*

4

3

PS156/IS392 further enhances the local community by providing for the area its main civic building. The common areas, including the auditorium, gymnasium, and cafeteria, are each located in a separate wing from the classroom wings, and can be used outside normal school hours.

The school is the recipient of funds from the New York Department of Cultural Affairs' Percentage for Art program that provided for a permanent, two-story, site-specific art installation by noted sculptor Ned Smyth. The artwork was commissioned to create an illuminated wall to appear as a beacon of light onto the playground. The entire project will serve as a beacon of hope for the neighborhood. The new school has instilled new life into the historically under-served Ocean Hill Brownsville community.

5 *Interior staircase showing art wall*

6 *Corridor*

7 *Library*

8 *Auditorium*

Photography: *Kevin Chu/KCJP*

5

6

7

8

Our Lady of Sorrows Elementary School
Toronto, Ontario, Canada
• Diamond & Schmitt Architects Incorporated

1

3

4

2

Our Lady of Sorrows Elementary School is connected to the Memorial Pool and Community Recreation Centre, completed three years earlier by Diamond & Schmitt Architects Incorporated. The pool, ice rink and activity room of the community complex can be assessed for use by the school children during the midday off-peak hours. Similarly, the school gymnasium can be used by the public in the evening when the school is not in use. The indoor link between the public school and community center is crossed by a public walkway and bikeway linking Montgomery Road to the valley lands of Mimico Creek.

The sloping landscape of the site was exploited in a split-level section through the school. Two classroom wings are a half-floor apart, thus facilitating movement by kindergarten- and primary-aged children. The classroom wings surround and overlook an interior court which connects directly to the exterior playground. This court is the heart of the school and provides a place for lunch, games, and gatherings of the student body,

>>

1 *View from pool*

2 *Front elevation*

3 *Stair*

4 *Central activity lunchroom*

MEDICAL AND SPECIAL ACCOMMODATION

Children's Medical Center of Dallas
Dallas, Texas, USA
• HKS, Inc.

The Children's Medical Center of Dallas addition includes more than 79 patient beds and a major expansion of the diagnostic/treatment areas. The additional beds are accommodated on three floors of 24-bed clusters and a 30-bed infant and pediatric intensive care unit.

The diagnostic/treatment areas include a major expansion of radiology to nine procedure rooms, cardiac catheterization, and the addition of heart and liver transplant operating rooms. The siting of the existing building, adjacent to the county hospital, promotes an image of a hospital designed to meet both children's and parents' needs.

1 *Train room*
2 *Lobby*
Photography: *Rick Grunbaum*

Children's Pavilion and Playground at La Rabida Children's Hospital

Chicago, Illinois, USA

• VOA Associates Incorporated Architecture / Planning / Interior Design

1

2

La Rabida Children's Hospital is a specialty children's hospital that provides comprehensive inter-disciplinary healthcare to chronically ill children. The hospital provides training and education for caregivers to creatively respond to the challenges of children with chronic illnesses, and their families. Located on a promontory on Lake Michigan, the site offers panoramic views of the lake and La Rabida's setting in Jackson Park. The hospital serves a heavily Medicaid-dependant population. Philanthropic support is paramount to fund the services the hospital provides to meet the ongoing health care needs of children.

A play environment incorporating play activities, rehabilitation programs for patients and leisure activities for the staff is housed in a new children's pavilion. All surfaces are wheelchair-accessible, and the play environment also accommodates patients in gurneys, on crutches, and those linked to mobile life-support systems. A portion of the play environment, dedicated to rehabilitation activities, is covered with a thick, resilient rubber system which allows for ground-level activities on a safe and comfortable surface. Because of the variety of rehabilitation programs, most equipment was not built in to allow the staff to bring out highly specialized equipment required for individual patients' needs. Adjacent to the rehabilitation area a small sunken theater was created to provide social learning activities.

Adjacent to the Children's Pavilion, a new therapeutic playground provides wheelchair-accessible play equipment in an active play area, new fountain and landscaping, and a special rehabilitative play area. The lakefront play area is protected by a new shoreline revetment in conjunction with walking and riding paths to provide safe, protected access to the lakeshore for patients and the surrounding community.

1 *Nautical-themed playground*
2 *Wheelchair access to children's playground*
3 *Wheelchair ramp with view to Lake Michigan*

3

Inpatient Addition to La Rabida Children's Hospital

Chicago, Illinois, USA

• VOA Associates Incorporated Architecture / Planning / Interior Design

When VOA was hired to plan and design the new inpatient 'wing' the project team understood that every dollar must count. The new beds were planned and built on an expanded roof of the Finnegan building. As part of the redevelopment, the project includes a new pair of hospital-sized elevators and new heating, ventilation, air conditioning, and an electrical system. Architectural design focused on creating a unified image for the hospital consistent with the character and style of the campus. While striving to make the most of the unique site of the hospital by the lake, the design uses materials, details, and architectural elements that will create a timeless and classic image.

The goal of the interior design was to create a child and family-centered environment. All patient rooms have rooming-in capabilities. The interior design follows previous designs of outpatient areas, which follow a nautical theme. The core of the new unit, called the S.S. La Rabida, is formed as a ship. Passenger 'cabins' (patient rooms) are located along the outside, and all services are arranged between the stern and the prow-shaped common play area. Each patient room has porthole-shaped vision panels in the doors. Wayfinding is based on a nautical flag system, and donor recognition has been planned into the design, given the importance of donations in the success of the project.

1

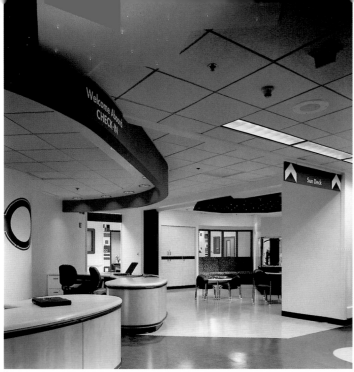

2

1 Donor recognition wall
2 Welcome aboard/check-in
3 Nurses' station and sun deck

3

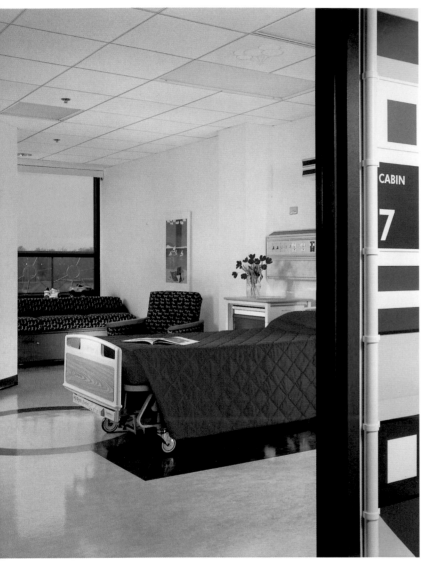

4

4 *Passenger cabin and room signage*

5 *Double passenger cabin*

6 *Passenger cabin accommodating patients and families*

Photography: *Hedrich-Blessing*

5

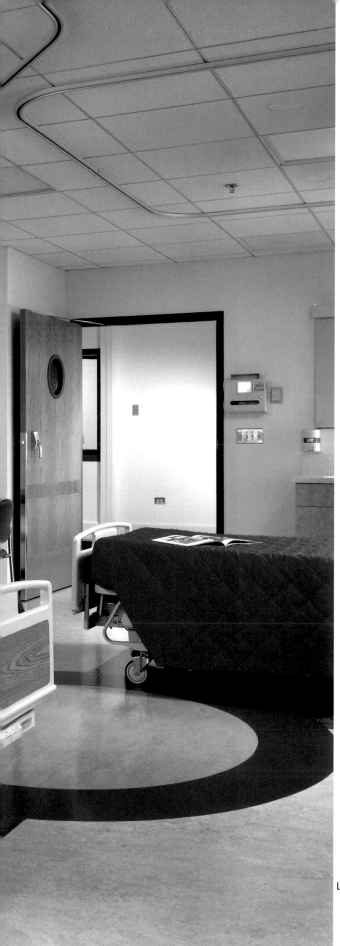

6

La Rabida Children's Hospital | VOA Associates Incorporated Architecture / Planning / Interior Design   67

The St. Vincent de Paul Center

Chicago, Illinois, USA

• VOA Associates Incorporated Architecture / Planning / Interior Design

1

The St. Vincent de Paul Center, owned and operated by the Daughters of Charity, is a new 12,500-square-meter childcare center located in the heart of Chicago's Lincoln Park. This nonprofit center serves an estimated 400 low-income, disadvantaged, and at-risk children. The building, primarily a daycare center, also provides outreach and educational programs for the homeless and senior citizens within the surrounding community.

When VOA first met with the Daughters of Charity, their existing 85-year-old building was expensive to operate, in need of renovation, too small for their needs, and didn't meet current building codes. The Daughters' took this opportunity to construct a new, modern, flexible building that not only met current codes and regulations, but provided an enriching environment for the children in their care.

VOA's design team conducted visioning sessions with staff, children, foster grandparents from the senior center, and members of the community in order to draw upon many different experiences of childhood for inspiration.

>>

1 *Playground and southern façade*

2 *Bay window with view onto playground*

2

3

The exterior of the building and the main lobby evoke the traditional spirituality of the Daughters of Charity and the nurturing stability of St. Vincent de Paul within the context of the neighborhood.

However, in the areas of the facility where children are the primary occupants, classrooms, corridors, and bathrooms, the scale of the fixtures, windows, and furniture are child-sized. The scale shifts depending on the age of the children who occupy each floor, from six months to ten years. Classrooms are divided into three areas: a quiet zone, including bay windows to the outside, activity zones in the center of each room, and wet zones where kids can be creative and messy and where the fixtures are scaled to smaller hands. This use of scale, combined with soft slopes, eye-level circular windows, soothing colors, and non-institutional materials such as plaster (which is friendlier than concrete and just as easy to clean) create an environment where children want to spend time and feel in control of their surroundings.

3 *Main lobby with stained-glass windows*
4 *Wet zone where kids can be creative*
5 *Corridor with child-size windows*
6 *Eye-level porthole window for children*

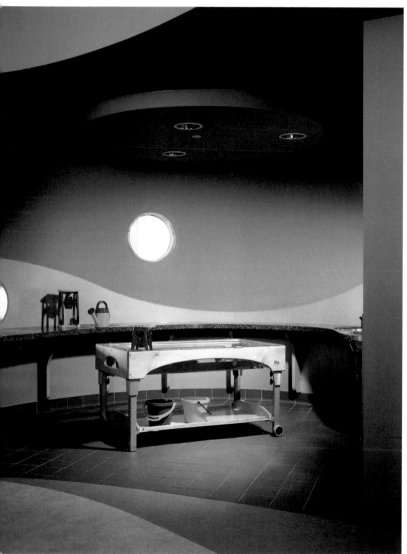

4

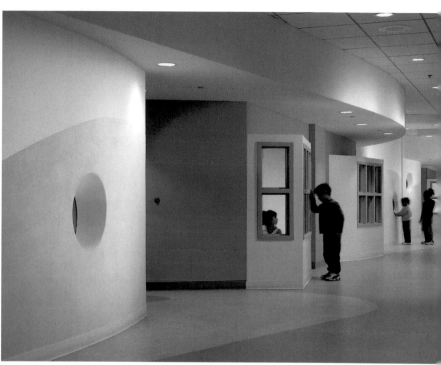

5

6

7

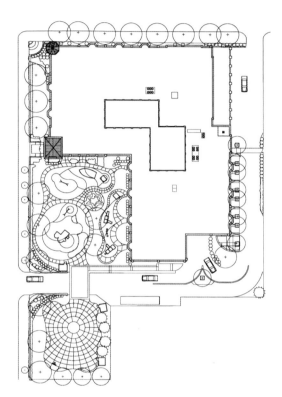

7 *Elevation*

8 *Floor plan*

9 *Nursery*

10 *Gymnasium*

11 *Classroom*

Photography:
*James Steincamp © Steincamp/Ballogg Chicago
(1,2&9); Hedrich-Blessing (3–6,10&11)*

9

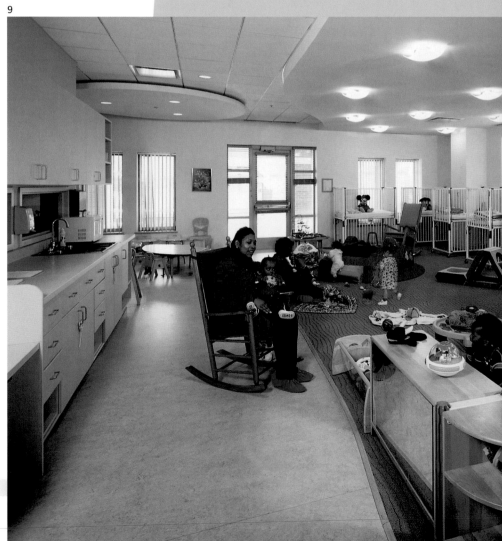

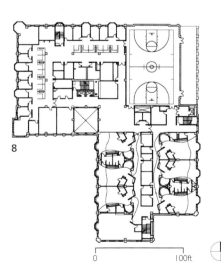

8

0   100ft

10

11

The St. Vincent de Paul Center | VOA Associates Incorporated Architecture / Planning / Interior Design   73

Family Life Center
Children's Memorial Medical Center
Chicago, Illinois, USA
• VOA Associates Incorporated Architecture / Planning / Interior Design

At Children's Memorial Medical Center, the VOA design team took an innovative approach to understanding children. They brought together children and their families, students from Texas A&M University, caregivers and design professionals. Chronically ill children and their families shared insight from their personal experience within the healthcare setting. Seventeen students presented findings on their extensive research within children's environments. Caregivers offered insight on their daily interactions with children and their families in the hospital setting. VOA's facility planners, architects and interior designers drew inspiration from the team, and began to dream of the possibilities for creative expression within the physical environment. Through extensive on-site charettes, the group began to develop ideas that truly reflected healthcare from a child's experience and perspective.

Traditionally, children's hospital environments have focused on creating a homelike and familiar environment. At Children's Memorial Medical Center, the team imagined 'what the hospital should be.' An innovative concept emerged, one that focused on discovery and imagination. These themes work into all aspects of design. The final result has a nautical theme.

1

2

The final product makes available to the family of a sick child, an office to catch up on work, padded benches, and places for play and relaxation. This refuge in a light well of leftover space between buildings is also the first articulation of the hospital's interiors master plan.

1 *Entry lobby with aquarium*

2 *Family room with books and magazines*

3 *'Under the Sea' corridor*

3

4

5

6

4 *Entry into play space*

5 *Children at play in atrium space*

6 *Atrium space and game wall*

Photography:
Doug Snower Photography

The Bristol-Myers Squibb Children's Hospital at Robert Wood Johnson University Hospital

New Brunswick, New Jersey, USA

• Shepley Bulfinch Richardson and Abbott
in association with Hillier Architecture

1

2

1 *Main entrance: welcoming canopy and entry pavilion engage children and families without excessive cuteness or condescension*

2 *Lively portion of Family Resource Center is geared specifically toward siblings and young patients*

3 *Nurses' station in pediatric intensive care unit: reception desk provides main focus at entrance of each unit*

4 *Main lobby: custom-designed stained glass and undulating soffit give waiting area playful atmosphere*

To increase and enhance its pediatric care services, Robert Wood Johnson University Hospital engaged SBRA, in association with The Hillier Group, to design a new children's hospital for its medical campus in downtown New Brunswick. The hospital supports 45 recognized pediatric specialties under the clinical leadership of the University of Medicine & Dentistry of New Jersey and the Robert Wood Johnson Medical School.

The six-story facility has a separate entrance and lobby to provide exclusive access to pediatric programs, while connecting to the existing main building for use of support services. The facility includes 13,560 square meters of new construction and renovation, housing, and replacement beds for use by various pediatric departments. Program elements include: surgery; adolescent hematology and oncology; pediatric intensive care—the only unit in the region; pediatric emergency room; Level 1 trauma center; expanded Child Life center; family center;

and resource center, which provides research materials and computers for patient and family use.

Visitors are greeted by the children's arrival garden with attractive landscaping, a fountain, trellises, and integrated lighting. The main lobby or entry pavilion then welcomes children with an interactive, educational play area. Patient floors include family support areas and outdoor play terraces. These design and program elements—and other operational efficiencies and accommodations throughout the building—reflect SBRA's concept of family centered design and show the hospital's commitment to creating a healing environment for the unique needs of children and their families.

3

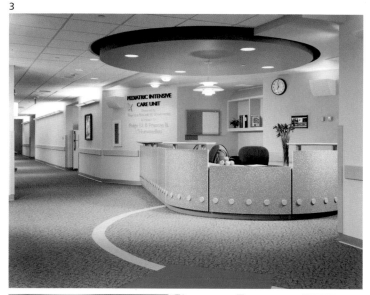

4

5

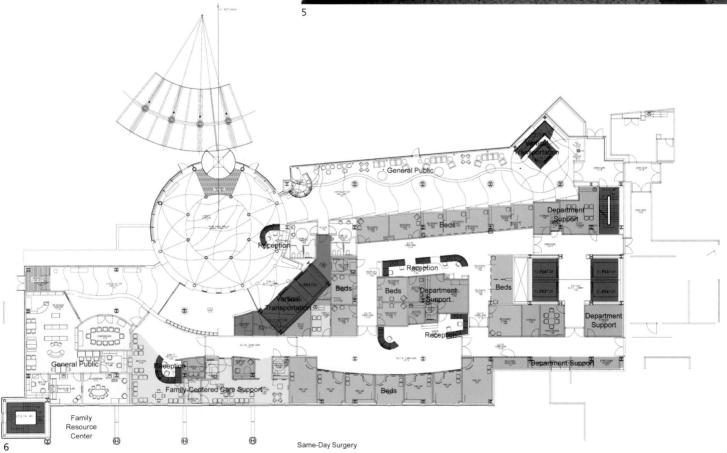

6

General Public

Vertical Transportation

Reception

Department Support

Reception

Beds

Beds

Beds

Department Support

Beds

Reception

Department Support

Vertical Transportation

General Public

Reception

Family-Centered Care Support

Family Resource Center

Department Support

Beds

Same-Day Surgery

5 *Play and lounge area: third-floor get-away space above entrance atrium gives families a relaxing break from medical environment*

6 *Floor plan/first floor*

7 *Floor plan/second floor*

Photography:
Barry Halkin (1, 3–5); Meg Shin (2)

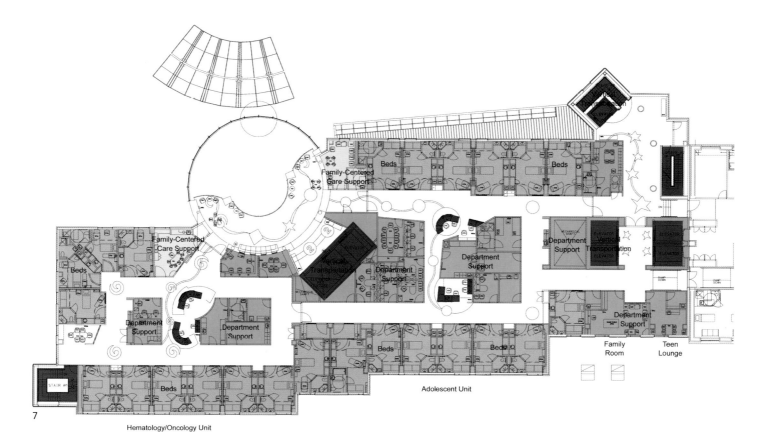

7

Hematology/Oncology Unit

Adolescent Unit

The Hasbro Children's Hospital at Rhode Island Hospital

Providence, Rhode Island, USA

• Shepley Bulfinch Richardson and Abbott

1

2

1 *Chalk boards and toys help create home-like atmosphere for younger patients*

2 *Entrance and secret garden make engaging first impression on younger patients*

3 *Playful sculpture and fanciful entrance enhance child-oriented atmosphere*

4&5 *'Backyard' playhouse subdivides clinic's central waiting area into four separate spaces, each with its own reception desk*

Photography: *Jean Smith*

This children's hospital integrates pediatric diagnostic and treatment functions with patient beds in a new building linked to a long-range facilities plan, which will connect major program elements of the Rhode Island medical complex and the nearby Medical Mall through a series of lobbies and atria.

Program elements include a 15-bed intensive care unit, physical therapy, and three 30-bed patient care bed floors divided by age. Surgery, emergency and radiology suites are located near adult services to provide flexible swing space. A double-height lobby links two major entrances and features a two-level playhouse, fountain, aquarium, and gift shop.

The cluster-like form of the inpatient units provides close proximity between care-giver, child, and family. It also permits sub-clustering of patients with different nursing needs and easy conversion to intensive care. Each patient floor is a 'neighborhood' for 30 children and their families, with playrooms,

4

5

activity area, and classrooms. Art is integral to the design, which includes an interactive granite fountain in the lobby, murals and sculptures in waiting areas, and ceramic tiles by local school children in corridors and at nurses' stations.

At ground level, the building houses a 2400-square-meter pediatric clinic with space for primary and adolescent care, specialty, and cancer units. The clinic provides a flexible arrangement of shared exam spaces arranged around a central waiting area with a two-story playhouse. An outdoor children's garden includes an interactive fountain, a walkway with trellises, and a picnic shelter.

3

New York University Child Study Center

New York, New York, USA

• Perkins Eastman

The New York University Child Study Center is a 1500-square-meter multidisciplinary facility housing programs focused on children's developmental, behavioral, and psychiatric issues. Conceived by celebrated child and adolescent psychiatrist Dr Harold Koplewicz, the center's mission goes beyond conventional treatment and family counseling and is dedicated to scientific research, clinical services, evaluation, and the development of new treatments.

Fitting spaces for outpatient clinical evaluation, research, and support services into the lower two floors of a new residential tower was a major challenge. Using architecture to support and enhance the therapeutic process was another. Creating a place that was both child and family friendly and that would appeal to both young children and adolescents was a third challenge.

1

2

3

4

5

1 *Research floor waiting area*

2 *Stairs to second floor*

3 *Patient waiting area*

4 *Main patient waiting area*

5 *Workstations*

6 *Main reception area*

7 *Research office*

Photography:
Chuck Choi Architectural Photography

The main entrance is at the corner of the building, leading into the evaluation area on the ground floor. Research spaces are on the second floor. A stair and an elevator at the entry provide easy access between floors.

The design models the examination room suite on a village or neighborhood, with many places for children to discover.

A large skylight located deep in the suite brings natural light into as many exam rooms as possible; each examination room also features a glazed clerestory to defuse any anxiety associated with psychiatric treatment. Lighting levels are low to create a more intimate atmosphere for patients and their families. The interior palette includes primarily warm, light-colored woods with cheerful accent colors.

6

7

New York University Child Study Center | Perkins Eastman   85

Bright Building at Children's Medical Center of Dallas

Dallas, Texas, USA

• HKS, Inc.

1

The Bright Building at the Children's Medical Center of Dallas houses the hospital's ear, nose, and throat programs—one of the largest such programs in the USA.

It is also home to the ARCH Center. The 7400-square-meter facility is built horizontally on a 300-meter tract of land. The building allows the consolidation of many services offered at the existing Children's Medical Center in Dallas.

The signature of the new facility is a one-of-a-kind 'planescape,' greeting children and their families as they enter the four-story atrium. A ceiling-suspended glider plane, provided by the Frontiers of Flight Museum at Love Field, serves as the planescape's centerpiece.

3

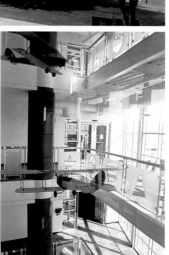

2

4

1 *Exterior of Bright Building*

2 *Four-story atrium greets families with inviting 'planescape'*

3 *Ceiling-suspended glider plane, provided by Frontiers of Flight Museum at Love Field, serves as planescape's centerpiece*

4 *Entry to Bright Building*

Photography: *King Graf*

Texas Scottish Rite Hospital for Children

Dallas, Texas, USA

• HKS, Inc.

HKS and Texas Scottish Rite Hospital for Children teamed up to design and build a specialty teaching hospital for children suffering primarily from both orthopedic disorders and learning disabilities.

The project also consisted of additional space for two parking structures, a separate power plant, and a bio-engineering research center.

HKS has worked with Scottish Rite Children's Hospital for over 30 years. Since that time, the firm has completed more than five projects including renovations and additions to keep in pace with the hospital's growth.

1

2

3

4

1&2 *Playful signage was designed at Texas Scottish Rite Hospital for Children in Dallas*

3 *Entry lobby*

4 *Waiting area*

Photography: *Steven Vaughn (1&2); Rick Grumbaum (3); Karen Snyder (4)*

Pediatrics Speciality Clinic at Remington Oaks

San Antonio, Texas, USA

• Marmon Mok: Architecture, MEP Engineering, Interior Design

Twenty-seven physicians came together to create a 2000-square-meter children's multi-speciality clinic. The designer was asked to create waiting area pavilions which would provide a learning environment for children served by the facility. 'Our Planet Earth' was selected as a theme for the three waiting rooms and elevator lobby.

Upon arrival at the elevator lobby, visitors are greeted by a carpet of stars within a swirling galaxy. From this vantage point the three waiting room pavilions, named Earth, Sky, and Water, are visible. Within the Earth pavilion, tall grasses surround the room with rhinos, elephants, and zebras peering through the leaves. A monkey and giraffe peer down over the reception desk concealed within a hut structure. The Sky pavilion features a pyramid skylight and weather mobile with rain, snow, and sunshine. A frieze of clouds and stars encircle and support the base of the skylight. Within the depths of the Water pavilion, sea turtles and dolphins swim among schools of fish. The walls alternate layers of aqua and teal and serve as backdrop to the tug boat reception desk. Marmon Mok's unique design transforms a child's visit into a friendly experience, which is certainly a departure from the traditional medical office.

1

2

3

1&3 *Reception area*
2 *Elevator lobby*
4 *Sea room waiting area*
Photography: *Paul Bardagjy*

4

NBA Tennyson Center for Children and Families at Colorado Christian Home

Denver, Colorado, USA

• Fentress Bradburn

2

1

3

1 *Varied façade of main entrance references surrounding neighborhood*

2 *Playful details include curved enclosure wall and tree-house-style suspended second floor*

3 *Ribbon theme was incorporated into soffits, lighting fixtures, and furniture*

4 *Dynamic details enliven this large multi-function room, currently configured as gymnasium*

5 *Multi-function room, currently configured as auditorium*

Photography: *Gordon Schenck (1&2); Nick Merrick (3–5)*

4

5

The NBA Tennyson Center for Children and Families at Colorado Christian Home was originally established in 1904 as an orphanage. Today, it's a non-profit organization that provides residential housing, therapy and education for emotionally, physically, and sexually abused children aged 5 to 12, as well as therapy for the children and their families.

When Fentress Bradburn was selected to design the new school and treatment facility, the client was considering purchasing new land and locating the facility remotely from the existing children's housing.

Through a master-planning process, several campus schemes were generated showing how the programmatic requirements could be accommodated within the existing site. This enabled substantial economic advantages to be realized, while also fulfilling the center's goals of 'unifying the child's experience of living, playing, healing and learning.'

Buildings where children live, play and go to school affect how they feel about themselves, their ability to communicate with others, and the image they project to society. Good buildings help evoke positive emotions. Winston Churchill's eloquent words, 'First we shape our buildings and thereafter they shape us,' inspired the design for the new NBA Tennyson Center for Children and Families. The campus is tied together with a common thread—a child's ribbon that architecturally and through the landscape design connects the many buildings on site with the new facility.

Child Assessment Unit, Cambridge Hospital

Cambridge, Massachusetts, USA

• Roth and Moore Architects

1

Designed and constructed within one wing of the seventh floor of an existing urban hospital, this children's psychiatric in-patient facility contains 12 beds in a mix of single and double rooms. The unit is an assessment and diagnostic facility serving children aged six to 14.

The high-security unit is designed to be self-contained with spaces for sleeping, eating, education, recreation, and therapy arranged according to daily routine. The center corridor, required by the existing structure, is viewed as the 'main street' of the unit, enlivened with alcoves and built-in seating, establishing a sense of place critical to the success of the department.

>>

1 *Activities room also serves as dining room*

Opposite *Each patient is provided with an open cubby unit for clothing and a stainless-steel mirror for dressing*

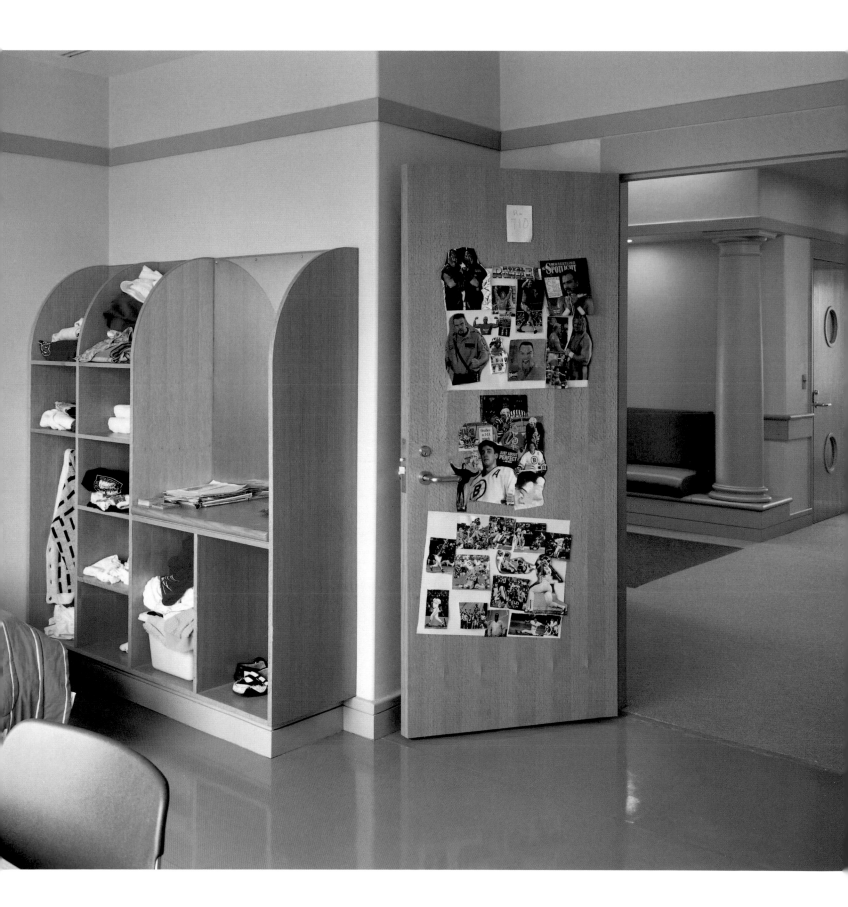

3

4

Throughout this unit an emphasis has been placed on de-institutionalizing the hospital environment through the careful selection of materials, colors, and finishes. The result is a durable, safe, and secure environment with a level of warmth and comfort that enhances the work of the unit.

5

6

3 *One of two classrooms providing individual instruction*

4 *Public lobby waiting area outside unit*

5 *Built-in seating enlivens Main Street*

6 *Floor plan*

Photography: *Steve Rosenthal*

Deerfield Elementary School
Deerfield, Michigan, USA
• Fanning/Howey Associates, Inc.

1

A unique, new 25,300-square-meter K–4 magnet facility, Deerfield Elementary School accommodates 500 students in two multi-grade neighborhoods. The neighborhoods are designed in a flexible, semi-open setting with large extended learning areas, or 'discovery' rooms that can be used for large and small group activities, special projects, access to technology resources, exhibits, and tutoring.

Locating the school at the perimeter of a wetland area provided many opportunities to support the school district's core vision to have the site and building design reflect the natural environment.

The concept of exploring this natural world is then expressed at the interior entrance to the Learning Center by a wooden bridge passing through a diorama, incorporating Michigan wetlands. The diorama is further amplified by a contiguous 11-meter-diameter domed ceiling, illuminated indirectly and painted to form a vast sky. Directly below the sky lies a carpet graphic of the earth's core and corresponding layers.

The Learning Center was designed to integrate the outside environment. Suspended white acoustical ceiling tiles are cloud-shaped with the surrounding exposed ceiling and upper wall surfaces painted in sky blue. Four acoustical murals representing each season border the room and maintain sound control within the voluminous space. A large-scale carpet graphic of the globe and phases of the sun and moon is centrally located to promote science and astronomy. Within the Learning Center is a reading and media room with a domed ceiling, which doubles as a planetarium in which to study the solar system.

A direct link is established to the exterior natural environment via a greenhouse space at the 'prow' of the Learning Center. Planting areas extend along each length of the greenhouse enclosure and additional wooden bridges pass through this nature area, connecting this interior space to the exterior learning courtyard on the edge of the wetland site.

2

1 *Learning Center entrance*

2 *Circular room with domed ceiling accommodates astronomy presentations*

3 *Flexibility is enhanced through use of movable bookshelves*

Photography:
Emery Photography, Inc.

3

3

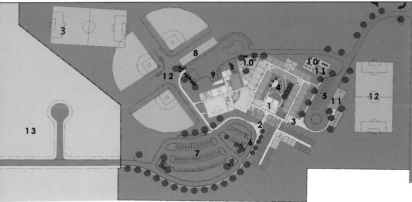

LEGEND:

1	New K-8 School	7	Staff Parking
2	Main Entry	8	Bus Garage
3	Bus Entry	9	Service Entry
4	Courtyard	10	Playground (soft surface)
5	Bus Loading	11	Playground (hard surface)
6	Parent Drop-off/	12	Play Fields
	Visitor Parking	13	Neighborhood

4

Acoustical treatments were incorporated as both functional elements and an opportunity to enliven the space with form and color. Several mounted panels feature bold geometric blocks. Circular speakers, a curved purple and white wall accent (which also serves an acoustical function), and bright red and apple green paint framing the stage also serve as vivid design elements. Suspended, triangular ceiling forms incorporate a subtle geometric pattern and house stage lights near the front of the room. A boldly striped linoleum floor and colorful chairs also brighten the space.

The new dining area met the district's goals in generating economical and functional design solutions that are also fun and attractive.

3 *Commons for dining and performance*

4 *Site plan*

Opposite *Main lobby and elementary school administration area*

Photography:
Emery Photography, Inc.

CULTURE

2

Draper Natural History Museum at the Buffalo Bill Historical Center

Cody, Wyoming, USA

• Fentress Bradburn

1

The Buffalo Bill Historical Center is widely regarded as America's finest Western-themed museum. Located in northwestern Wyoming on a bluff overlooking the Shoshone River, it is 84 kilometers from Yellowstone National Park's East Gate. The Draper Museum of Natural History joins the center's four internationally acclaimed museums—the Whitney Gallery of Western Art, the Buffalo Bill Museum, the Plains Indian Museum, and the Cody Firearms Museum—as the final element in a comprehensive portrayal of the West.

The design solution for the Draper Museum is responsive to program, sympathetic to context and distinctive in expression. While the Draper Museum wing mirrors the Firearms Museum in plan and elevation, its circular form creates an embracing effect at the front door drop-off and provides a counter element to the center's otherwise linear massing. The interior space is akin to a smaller version of the Guggenheim Museum in New York, with four quadrants that cascade vertically down from the main level to the lower level. The levels are developed in response to the Yellowstone area's natural habitat from Alpine at the top, through Forest and Meadow, to Plains at the bottom level.

>>

1 *Overall exterior with entrance to Buffalo Bill Historical Center (right) and Draper Museum wing (left)*

2 *Detail of Draper Museum wing with sunrise reflection*

6

Opposite *Intergalactic, inspirational journey awaits children aged 5–7 in 3-2-1 Penguins™*

6 *Working farm: two-year-olds cultivate their spiritual awareness in warm atmosphere, complete with picket fence and full-size cow plus cornucopia of hands-on activities*

Children beg to return each weekend. Since its opening, children's attendance figures have increased over 60 percent. Over 800 children fill the new center's 1500 square meters of interactive themed environments, offering families an innovative way to promote religious and spiritual awareness in ways which are culturally relevant to children.

The community entrusted the design team to create a world-class facility—one that would stray far from the typical Sunday school with its ubiquitous and dreary multipurpose classrooms. Instead, five differently themed environments were designed. Each is appropriate for a specific age and purpose, and includes the nursery, where infants and toddlers focus on the high contrast trains and manipulative landscape; two-year-olds work the farm and harvest the crops; preschoolers wriggle through drainage pipes with Noah's building plans; kindergarten through second-graders take off on an intergalactic mission of 'parable' proportion;

>>

The Randall Museum Theater

San Francisco, California, USA

• ELS Architecture and Urban Design
with Marcy Li Wong, Architect

1

2

This project is part of a 25-year master plan which ensures the development of a theater, gallery, and spaces for animal studies, crafts, and natural history. The first phase was the redevelopment of the original 200-seat auditorium which was built in 1951.

The architects transformed the existing plain concrete shell, complete with its poor sightlines, bad acoustics, lack of sound equipment, and fixed seating space, into a state-of-the-art live performance theater.

The ELS Architecture and Urban Design plan raised the floor and included newly constructed steeply tiered seating to improve sightlines. Acoustics were improved by isolating the existing mechanical unit above the stage, and by introducing a plenum in front of the stage area, linacoustic sound insulation on the walls, and carpeting on the floors and seats.

The stage was expanded outward onto the raised floor. Benches and movable chairs accommodate an increased audience of 250, and the new flexible seating can accommodate programs for children, adolescents, and adults, from full-scale productions to more intimate plays, lectures, music recitals, and educational training.

>>

3

4

1 *Auditorium before renovation— concrete shell lacked architectural interest*

2 *Auditorium before renovation*

3 *Benches and chairs accommodate an audience of 250*

4 *Renovated theater energized by seating and bright finishes*

5 *Foyer beyond newly raked seating*

6 *Lighting and acoustical grid adorns existing concrete shell*

5

6

Chicken Shed Theatre

London, UK

• Arts Team @ RHWL

1

The Chicken Shed is a theater workshop where people of all ages and abilities come together to develop skills in performing arts. What sets it apart is that 20 percent of its members have the kind of difficulties that would normally exclude them from this kind of activity.

The first phase, completed in 1994, produced an identifiable home for the company, complete with auditorium, workshop, and rehearsal studio.

The second phase extension and new interior works, funded through an Arts Council lottery grant, contains a new studio performance space and additional rehearsal and support areas, including workshops and recording rooms. The completed building, with its timber-decked landscape garden, provides the group with a vibrant and uplifting space in which to work.

The building enables the company to create, rehearse, and perform in one place, and provides a base for its outreach, education, and touring activities.

3

2

1 *Theater garden*

2 *View toward foyer*

3 *Performance space*

Photography: *John Walsom*

5

The interiors of the Exploration Station continue the philosophy by providing varied, well-lit volumes with visual and physical connections to the immediate landscape and exterior play areas. The new building includes three major halls for permanent and traveling exhibits, multipurpose areas, and a museum store. Each space provides a unique setting for a variety of exhibit types and experiences, including a multi-level castle with views out of the building's cupola. Interfacing the architecture of the building with the conceptual exhibit design creates a versatile and unique dynamic, and an integrated whole.

Opposite *Children adore 'Lucky Charm' windows and recognize that the building was designed for them*

5 *Fun, cut-out reception desk greets all visitors*

Photography:
Doug Snower Photography

6

7

the children. The design team studied these kid-generated images, met with staff, outside arts, education and science advisors. Design alternatives resulted for each floor of the new facility, followed by in-depth communication about the museum's future operational, aesthetic, and design needs for young visitors.

From kids' drawings to delightful design, phase one takes advantage of existing features such as high ceilings and concrete framing. To these pragmatic necessities, the architectural and exhibit design overlap to add a lively sense of color, dramatic variations in scale, with places to see things from different perspectives, and personalizing the dynamic structure. New interior columns even reach like children's outstretched arms propping up the building—the whimsical result of new structural bracing.

For an institution, which kindles curiosity and creativity, it is critical that the architecture also provides stimulation and excitement. The museum has been awarded the AIA Chicago Distinguished Building Award.

8

9

11

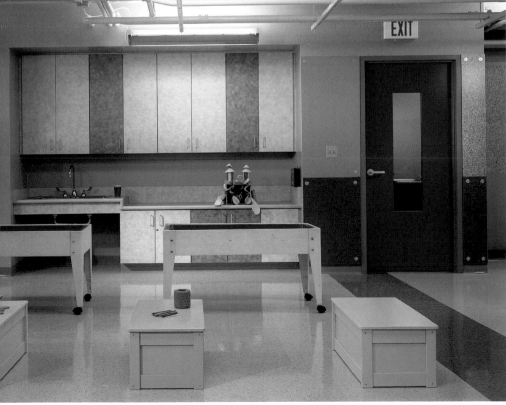

10

6 *Emma pops up underneath WaterWays, wet with fun*

7 *Brightly striped entry hall gives children clues to navigate the building with confidence*

8 *Children and families blown away by AirWorks*

9 *Children can build and invent using real tools and materials*

10 *Kids Discover Engineering labs or classrooms*

11 *Airworks and Waterways are favorite exhibits*

Photography:
Doug Snower Photography

ACTIVITY AND MULTI-PURPOSE

Marjorie Hilliard Hodges Children's Pavilion
Silver Bay, New York, USA
• Bohlin Cywinski Jackson

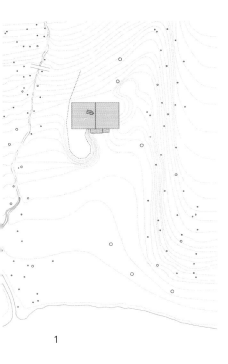

1

The Silver Bay Association is a non-profit organization, which for nearly 100 years has operated a retreat and conference center on Lake George in the Adirondack Mountains. The heritage-listed campus consists of 65 buildings on 250 hectares.

The Children's Pavilion was constructed on an exceptionally tight budget, yet it has a variety of indoor and outdoor spaces for children. Intended to serve very young children from infants to five-year-olds, the building's flexibility encourages its use by groups of all ages. The 280-square-meter interior is seasonally extended by an additional 170 square meters of porches, which provide protection from both the intense sun and frequent Adirondack showers. As an overall strategy, Bohlin Cywinski Jackson designed a rather simple rectangular pavilion with a gabled roof framed by economical residential wood trusses.

>>

1 Site plan

2 Center enclosed in simple rectangle retaining light-hearted feel

3 Porch

2

3

The roof trusses are supported by an edge beam that rings the building and a wood and steel composite beam that extends through the center. This visually rich roof framing is revealed at the heart of the pavilion, leading from its entry to a gathering/reading/skit area that projects from the pavilion's face toward the lake, and the early morning sun. The entry face is calm and strangely classical while the face toward the lake is playful. The plan can be freely shaped to the children's varied needs beneath this simple roof.

A rich variety of columns supports the pavilion. The porches of the entry face are marked by a series of round, tapered wood columns ordered from a catalogue. Simplified through the removal of the usual bases and capitals, they speak of the past and allude to historic buildings nearby. The pavilion's roof edge at another play porch is supported by economical 4x4 wooden columns that also provide the framework for a whimsical lattice, producing animated shadows.

At the light-filled gathering/reading space, the perimeter beam is supported by a pair of peeled tree trunks from the area's forest. These natural columns inhabit the storytelling space like people. The roof shedding of this space is supported by playfully tilted, slender steel pipe columns. The central beam is supported by a line of paired, milled timber columns that are visually married to the beam, and mark the pavilion's center.

4

5

6

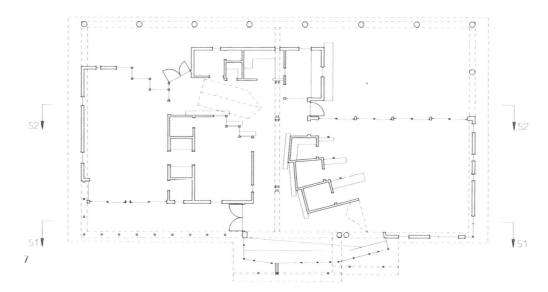

7

8

9

10

4&5 *Exposed structural elements in lobby*

6 *Ample porch space allows programs to extend outdoors during summer months*

7 *Building plan*

8 *Entry to reading room*

9 *Reading room*

10 *Spaced intermediate support columns*

Photography: *Karl Backus*

Kids on the Fly at O'Hare International Airport/Chicago Children's Museum

Chicago, Illinois, USA

• ArchitectureIsFun, Inc.

1

O'Hare International Airport in Chicago might be the world's busiest airport, yet included in its extensive network of elegant terminals and lounges is a space in which children are entertained and encouraged to interact and learn. On offer is a playful study of the local environment and the air transport industry.

The play facility is actually a satellite campus of the Chicago Children's Museum. The program called for a dynamic, safe, and secure environment to replicate in miniature the quality and mission of the museum, and to set a new standard for stand-alone exhibits. Beyond acting as a welcome relief from airport delays and stopovers, the satellite campus is envisioned as one of a series of cultural destinations and amenities intended to enhance and encourage use of the airport.

The design combines a variety of multi-sensory experiences in an appropriately scaled environment, which celebrates air travel in the context of Chicago and the world's busiest airport. Visitors can load cargo, re-fuel or even sit in the cockpit of a specially designed cargo plane. Children can also observe, monitor and listen to the activities at O'Hare via electronic interactives in a simulated control tower. A fantasy helicopter lets children's imaginations soar. An activity center provides opportunities to explore Chicago and the airport through a series of interactive exhibits developed by a collaboration of Museum and Department of Aviation staff. Under the shadow of a giant Lego Sears Tower, children can even re-plan downtown Chicago using Duplo blocks. An AIA Chicago Interior Architecture Award Winner, Kids on the Fly sets standards for airports everywhere by providing safe, accessible experiences for young travelers.

2

1 *Play is welcome respite for little travelers*

2 *Kids on the Fly is an accessible flight for all*

3 *Slide into fun: exhibit seems to be right on airfield*

4 *Right next to real gates, Kids on the Fly is true celebration of air travel*

Photography:
Doug Snower Photography (1&4); Howard Green (2&3)

3

4

Playmaze

Early Learning Exhibit at the Chicago Children's Museum
Chicago, Illinois, USA
• ArchitectureIsFun, Inc.

A fanciful miniature metropolis, Playmaze encourages a child's imagination through cognitive, social, and physical skills in a context-rich and integrated environment. Using the urban context as a theme, Playmaze offers visitors at the Chicago Children's Museum at Navy Pier a 150-square-meter space dedicated to early childhood development.

Specially designed for children up to six years of age and their caregivers, Playmaze is designed as a colorful city teeming with activity and opportunities for fun and learning. Exploring familiar places and everyday objects, the exhibits demystify daily experiences from which children are usually sheltered. Incorporating role-playing and interaction with adults, Playmaze assists children in their development of a sense of ownership, attachment, security, and place identity to the world around them.

1 *Playmaze is a mini metropolis of fun*

2 *Streets that toddlers can easily navigate on their own*

3 *Tot Lot*

4 *Bakery*

5 *Children can maintain their car in the garage*

Photography:
Doug Snower Photography

3

5

4

The city in movement, work, play, and rest beckons as the child and caregiver enter through a controlled gate expressing the uniqueness of the space.

Toddlers can drive a replica of a city bus, or change the tires and license plates on the Playmaze automobile. Donning waterproof smocks, they can use squeegees at the car wash, or pump gas and rebuild a motor to see how pieces fit together at the gas station. Tot Lot, a secure area with a 'peek-a-boo' bench, offers more privacy and shelter from the bustle of activity.

Play stations, such as a bakery fully stocked for baking, selling, and packaging, offer opportunities for 'city work' and adventure using a broad range of sensory perceptions.

Urban Youth Activity Center, LA County Sheriff's Youth Foundation

Los Angeles, California, USA

• Shubin + Donaldson

Making spaces for urban children to play has been a challenge for city administrators the world over. Los Angeles architects Shubin + Donaldson have been involved in a program to recycle decommissioned city buildings into spaces that respond to the community needs of children in urban environments. The result is an oasis where latch-key kids can do homework, play basketball and generally keep out of harm's way under the supervision of the LA County Sheriff's Youth Foundation.

From the crumbling foundations of empty government buildings, the LA County Sheriff's Youth Foundation saw a potential for change. Drawing on funding for construction from Time Warner and the Irmas Family, and buildings donated by LA County, Shubin + Donaldson were asked to plan and build an educational and recreation facil-

ity where neighborhood youth could access a library, classrooms for tutoring, sports activities, and nourishment, at the same time becoming familiar with law enforcement personnel. With tight budgetary constraints, the architects designed a complex that fulfills the multiple-use parameters. The buildings are also the most colorful place on the block, with rich green, yellow, and red paints chosen to accent the rather pedestrian government-owned building blocks.

The architects were also involved in raising funds for the project by obtaining donations of building materials from local suppliers. Corrugated metal paneling, rubberized flooring material, metal roll-up doors, particle board and a chain-link fence help provide a fortress-like façade to help protect the building and its users.

4

5

1 *Basketball is an important after-school activity*

2 *Existing structure is reused as youth center*

3 *Bright graphics inform neighborhood of new use*

4 *Chain link guards against graffiti*

5 *Young kids interact with playground*

Photography: *John Ford*

The Raccoon Club
St Louis, Missouri, USA
• John Guenther AIA of Mackey Mitchell Associates

1

This clubhouse, named the Raccoon Club by its occupants, is both a fun place for children to play, dream, and observe nature, and a contemplative retreat for the whole family.

Located in Ozark forest, it meets the request for a two-story lookout tower with a drawbridge.

The first floor is a mere 2.5 by 2.5 meters, complete with corner seats and an access ladder to the upper level. The upper level expands to 2.5 by 4.3 meters due to the sloping deck which projects outward to form a reclining seatback. A barrel-vault roof of clear polycarbonate plastic sheets provides protection and views upward to swaying trees, falling leaves, and rain drops, while filtering the light.

The upper level vantage point provides beautiful views of the surrounding forest: down to the tops of the dogwoods, across to the sassafras trees, and upward to the mighty oaks. The clubhouse also provides an ideal spot to watch the wildlife which passes through from an adjacent wildlife refuge.

The all-wood structure is classically composed. Its 'rusticated' base is made of stained skirt boards spaced to allow ventilation. The tower 'shaft' is clad in cedar shingles with the 'capital' defined by the splayed top. Large screened openings provide ample cross ventilation and framed views of the forest. The upper level is open and expansive, while the lower level is more closed and inward focused.

2

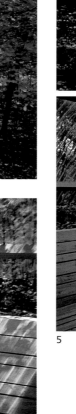

3

4

5

1&4 *Raccoon club with drawbridge*

2 *Stained skirt boards and cedar-shingle cladding*

3 *Sloping deck on upper level forms reclining seatback*

5 *Barrel-vaulted roof offers protection and views*

Photography: *John C. Guenther, AIA*

4

5

6

4 *Exterior view of underground home showing truncated cones*

5 *Cross section*

6 *Etched glass of 'pirates and indians'*

Photography: *James Morris*

Toyamma Children's Center

Isui-gun, Toyama Prefecture, Japan
• Environment Design Institute

Located in the center of a comprehensively planned park, this facility combines the kind of 'hands-on' exhibits found in many international children's museums, with the kind of creative, activity-oriented children's facilities common in Japan.

Divided into three levels, the first comprises an activity space fostering creativity, the second a 'hands-on' exhibition space, and the third a play space featuring a 100-meter-long play apparatus. Aiming to create space in which children would find it easy to play, it is shaped like a figure eight. The roof of the building provides the chance to survey the surrounding area.

2

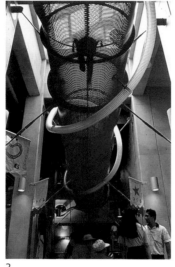

3

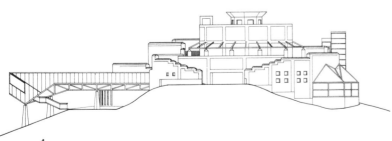

4

5

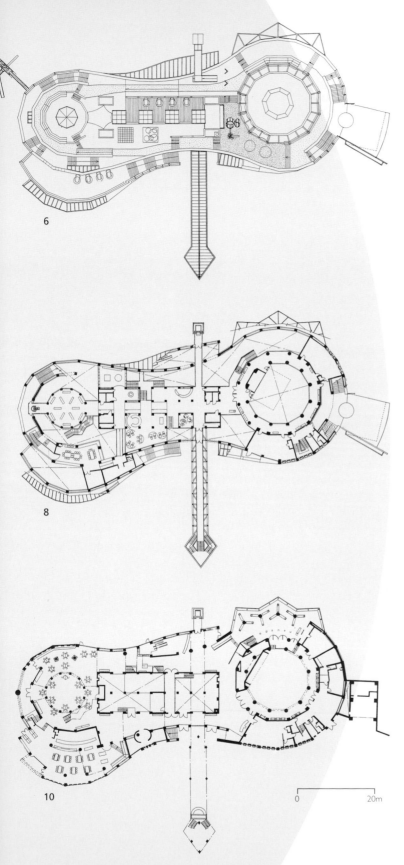

6

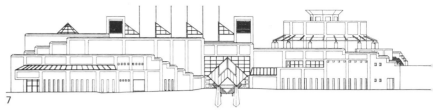

7

9

8

10

0   20m

1 Play space on roof

2 100-meter play tunnel
   suspended from ceiling

3 View from north

4 Southeast elevation

5 Play spaces under play tunnels

6 Third floor plan

7 Front elevation

8 Second floor plan

9 Suspended yellow play tunnel

10 First floor plan

Photography: *Mitsumasa Fujitsuka*

1

Kainan Wanpaku Park
Kainan City, Wakayama Prefecture, Japan
• Environment Design Institute

1 *Sliding on grass parkland*
2 *Looking up 'Tornado' net play structure*
3 *Section of Kazenoko tower*
4 *View of Kazenoko tower from grass parkland*
5 *Site plan*
6 *Spiral net and elevator for children to go up and down*
7 *'Step' tube play structure*
8 *Kazenoko theater on first floor*
Photography: *Mitsumasa Fujitsuka*

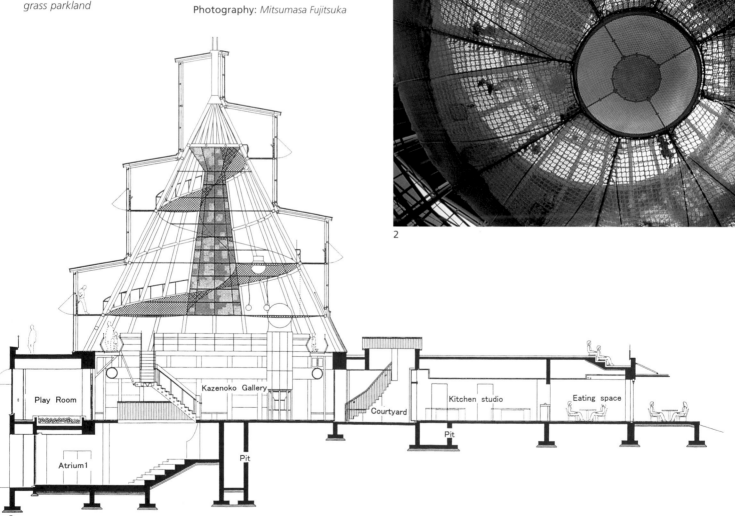

2

3

4

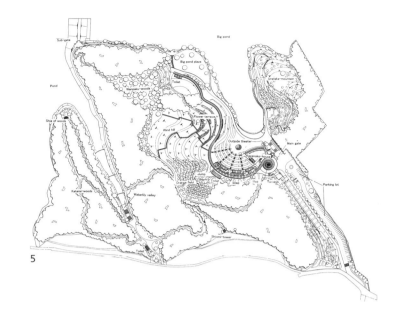

5

6

7

8

Located on the roof of the children's center, this tower play structure takes on a symbolic aspect while providing a skylight function.

The spiral tower is comprised of two major elements.

One is the spiral ramp that allows a splendid view while climbing or descending. The other is the interior with its nets, ropes, and other play items in the same spiral.

One of the camp's most popular attractions is a creative play area that incorporates existing trees, topographic variation, and natural rock outcrops as part of the play experience. This portion of the camp uses custom-designed and vendor-supplied equipment to provide a variety of climbing, sliding, jumping, running, discovery, and learning opportunities for campers of all ages. The design of all materials and colors was intended to harmonize with the existing woodland setting of Camp Hillard.

7

9

6

8

6 *Climbing wall mimics Camp Hillard's natural rock outcrops*

7 *Putting instruction on thematic miniature golf course*

8 *All play surfaces are natural wood chips or recycled rubber*

9 *Campers and leader testing flexible bridge*

10 *Coaching on child-scaled tennis courts*

11 *Young campers learn diving technique in 25-meter pool*

Photography:
Irvin Simon Photographers

10

11

1

Leipzig Swimming Pool
Leipzig, Germany
• Behnisch, Behnisch & Partner

2

Leipzig's new swimming pool complex imparts an abstract notion of combining sky and water—as with flying, and sea-diving birds like puffins and loons—presenting a playful, welcoming signal to the children who swim there. The pool is located near schools, playing fields, and the Stuttgarter Allee, a busy pedestrian street. Behnisch, Behnisch & Partner had previously designed a new park planned for a site behind the building. The new swimming hall was required to open up to this park, as well as fit comfortably into the existing city matrix. Inside, there are pools for sports, children's play, and lessons, as well as whirlpools and a sauna equipped to accommodate

3

4

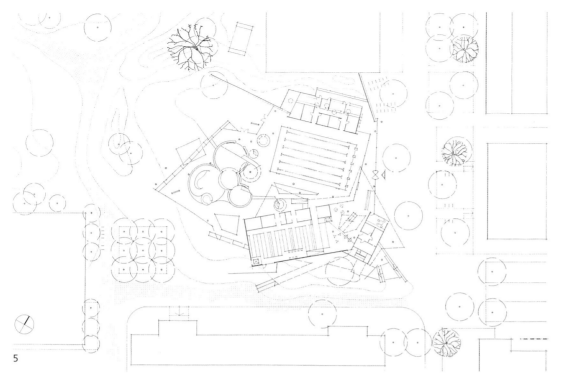

5

1 Vibrant color is used throughout the space

2 Signage seems to 'float' on glass

3 The facility is a comfortable, secure place for families

4 Variety of pools for children's play, sport, and lessons

5 Swimming hall opens to park and fits with existing city matrix

6 Sun streams in through ribbed-glass roof sections

7 Aircraft hangar effect suggests sky as well as water

Photography: Christian Kandzia/ Behnisch, Behnisch & Partner

40 people. The café terrace sits on a hill allowing a complete view of the city. The facility is a comfortable, secure place for families and individuals of all ages, and is an integral part of the community throughout the year.

The architects centered the design on the idea of openness. The façades of the swim hall are transparent, allowing a view from the Stuttgarter Allee, through the swim hall, and to the park. The idea of openness is conveyed through views: whether inside or out, views of and from the busy pedestrian street, the pools, or the terraced café, add dynamism to the building, and a sense of place to the site.

7

6

Leipzig Swimming Pool | Behnisch, Behnisch & Partner   171

INDEX